Notespeller for Piano

Book 2

A Visit to *Piano Park*
with Spike and Party Cat

Author
Karen Harrington

Director,
Educational Keyboard Publications
Margaret Otwell

Editor
Carol Klose

Illustrator
Fred Bell

FOREWORD

The **Notespeller for Piano** presents note recognition activities that coordinate with the **Piano Lessons** books in the **Hal Leonard Student Piano Library**.

Students join *Spike*, *Party Cat*, and friends as they enjoy rides and games at *Piano Park*. Their visit includes assignments that help students use the musical alphabet to read and write notes on the staff, identify intervals, and write sharps and flats.

Best wishes,

Karen Harrington

Karen Harrington

ISBN 978-0-634-01283-9

HAL•LEONARD®
CORPORATION
7777 W. BLUEMOUND RD. P.O. BOX 13819 MILWAUKEE, WI 53213

Visit Hal Leonard Online at
www.halleonard.com

At the Ticket Booths

When Spike and Party Cat arrive at *Piano Park*, they can buy admission tickets at the **Bass F** booth, **Middle C** booth, or **Treble G** booth.

Draw a line from each ticket to its booth below.

Piano Park Tokens

Spike and Party Cat are eager to begin their fun-filled day! Everyone entering the park receives tokens for rides and games.

Write the names of the notes on each token.

Use with Lesson Book 2, pg. 2

The Half-Note Express

Spike and Party Cat decide to ride the Half-Note Express. The train will take them past every ride in the park. Before boarding, they decorate each car with half notes.

1. Draw a half note one step down from the note printed on each car.
2. Write the note names in the blue boxes on each car.

The Train Ride

Name these notes to complete the story.

Use with Lesson Book 2, pg. 6

The Canoe Ride

Complete the story below by writing the note names in the blue boxes.

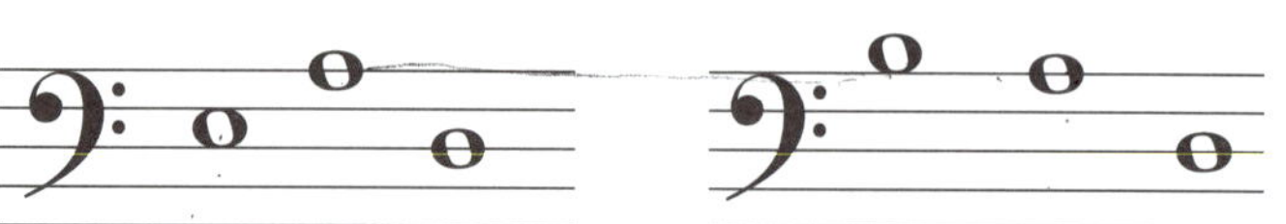

The canoes were r **e a d** y to **b o a r d** . Party Cat and Spike

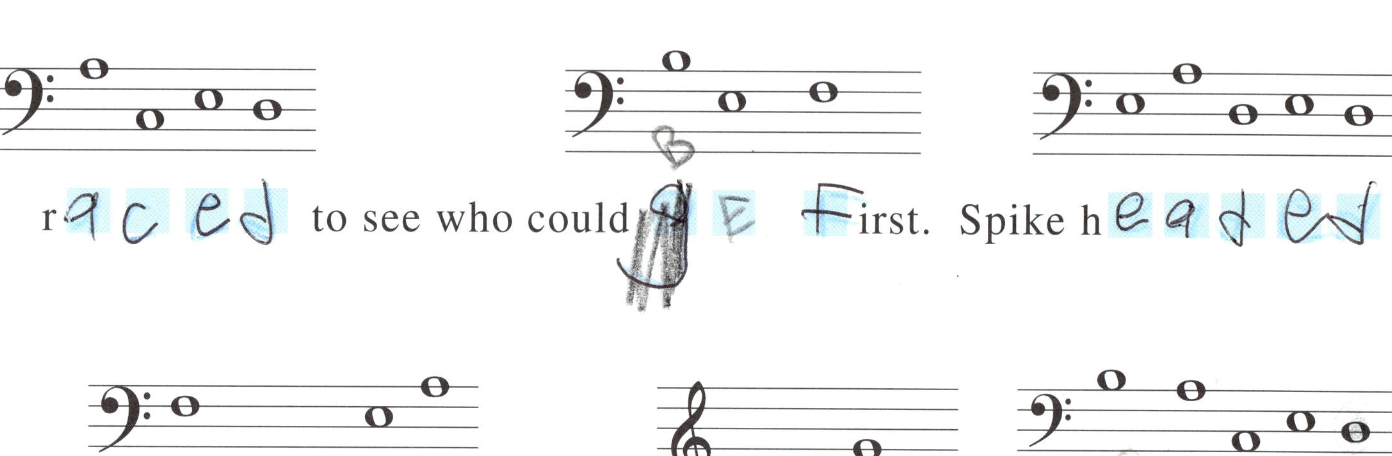

r **a c e d** to see who could **B E** **F**irst. Spike h **e a d e d**

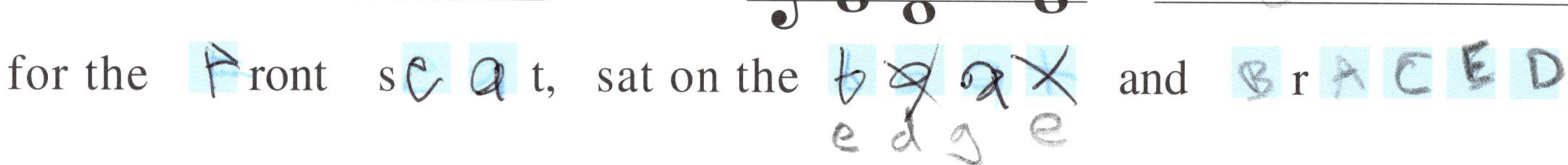

for the **F**ront s **c a** t, sat on the **b a x** (edge) and **B r A C E D**

himself for an **A D** v **e** nture . Cat sat in back, **r** ☐☐☐☐☐

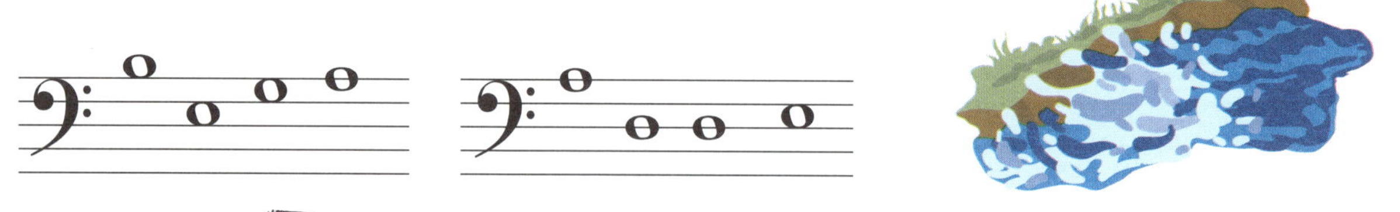

the oar and ☐ **C E F** n to p ☐☐ l through the rapids. Spike

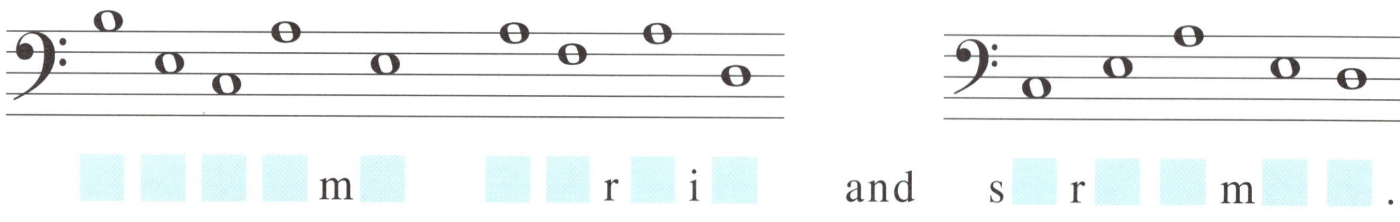

☐☐☐☐ m ☐☐ r ☐ i and s ☐ r ☐ m .

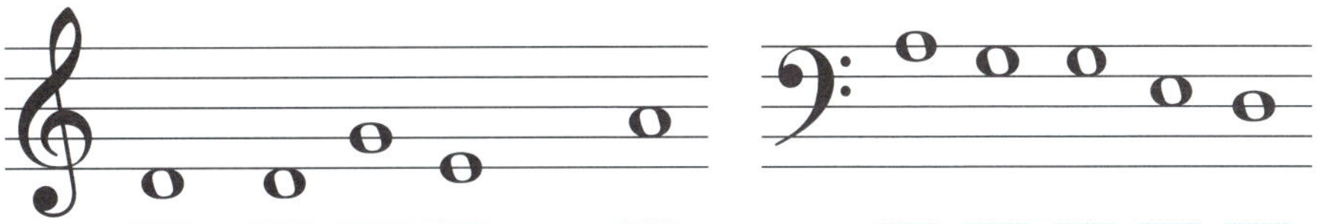

Cat had to o   j   log, but  r about his skill an□ r v ry.

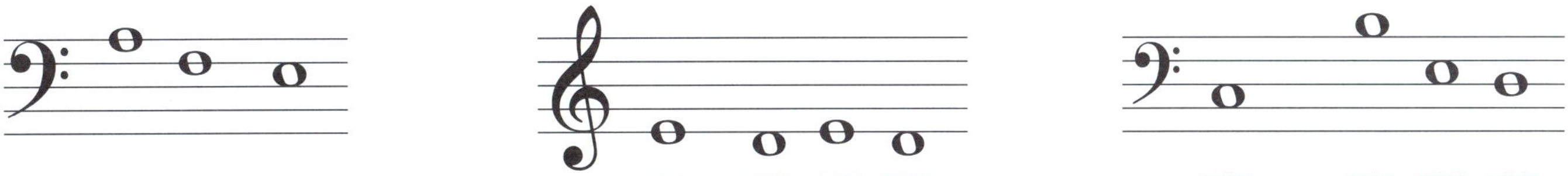

 t r the ride n , they lim 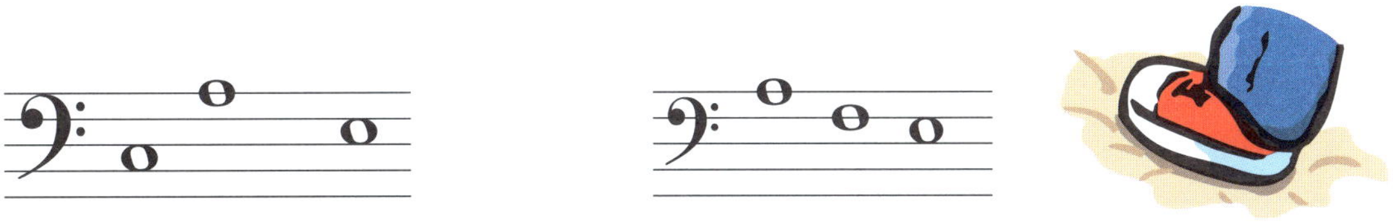 out of the c a no e onto a s , sandy 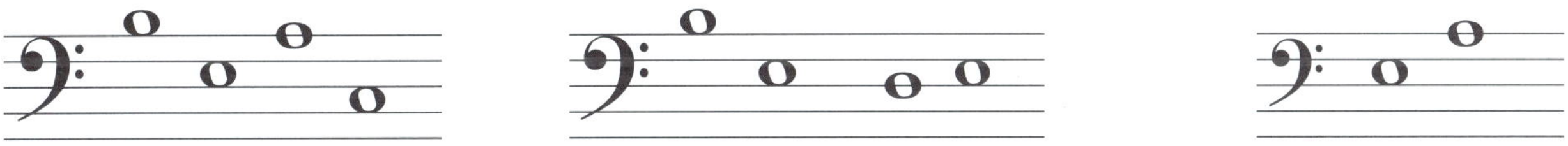 h si the str e a m.

Name the Canoes!

The canoe ride is a main attraction at *Piano Park*.
Write the names of the notes below to discover the names of the canoes.

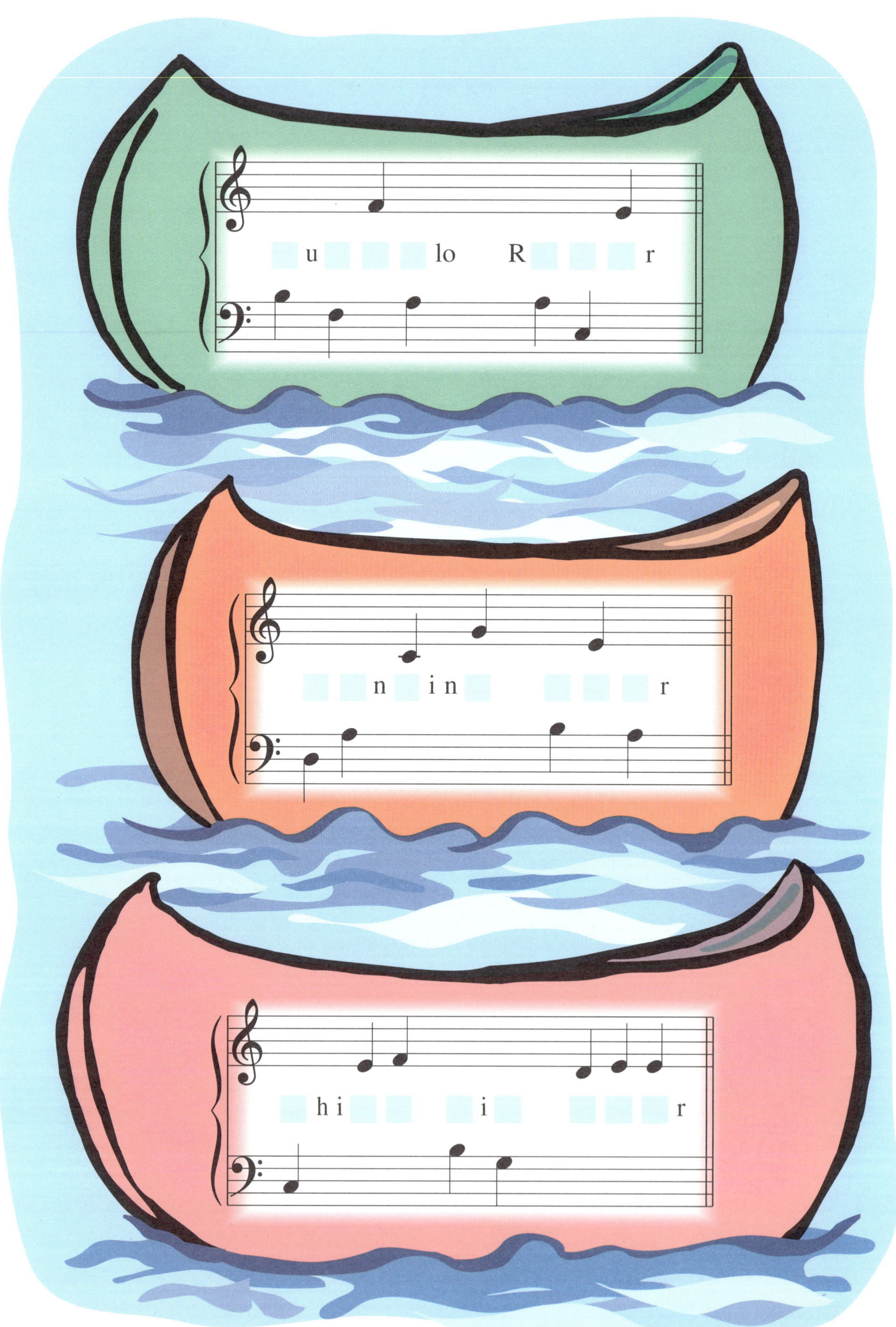

The Ferris Wheel

Party Cat and Spike think riding the ferris wheel is great fun. They love to go around and around, high above the ground!

1. Circle the correct interval in each example.
2. In the blue boxes, write the names of the notes.
3. Draw a straight line from each seat to the seat with the same notes on the opposite staff.

Use with Lesson Book 2, pg. 10

Snow Cones

After riding the ferris wheel, Spike and Party Cat meet Bear and Badger. They all stop to buy snow cones, Spike's favorite treat.

1. Name each note on the snow cones below.
2. Follow the clues at the bottom of the page to find out which flavor each friend chose.

Spike chose the flavor with 2nds.

Party Cat chose the flavor with 3rds.

Bear chose the flavor with 4ths.

Badger chose the flavor with repeated notes.

_______________   _______________   _______________   _______________

A Treasure Hunt

Bear and Spike decide to try their luck at the treasure hunt game.

1. Follow the interval clues and write the note-name answer on each clue.
2. To discover the prize, write the letter from each clue in the corresponding blank in the treasure chest at the bottom of the page.

Use with Lesson Book 2, pg. 13

The Airplane Ride

Complete the story by filling in the names of the notes.

In the blanks below, write the letters that have the same numbers in the story to find out what Party Cat lost.

$\overline{}$ $\overline{}$ $\overline{}$ $\overline{}$ $\overline{}$ $\overline{}$ $\overline{}$ $\overline{}$ $\overline{}$ $\overline{}$
1   2   3   4   5   6   7   8   9   10

The Magic Show

Spike and Party Cat notice a magician entertaining a crowd. Suddenly Spike exclaims, "Look! He just pulled your sunglasses out of his hat." Party Cat runs up to the magician, who hands the glasses to him with a deep bow. "That was really magic!" said Cat. "Let's stay and see what else he has in that hat."

The items the magician pulls from his hat are listed below each staff.
1. In the words below each staff, circle all the letters that are part of the musical alphabet.
2. On the staff, draw a quarter note for each letter you circled, placing the stems in the right direction.

Go Carts
A Rhyming Story

Spike and Party Cat couldn't wait to try the go carts!
Fill in the note names to complete the poem.

o   rts r   in   'round the tr   k,

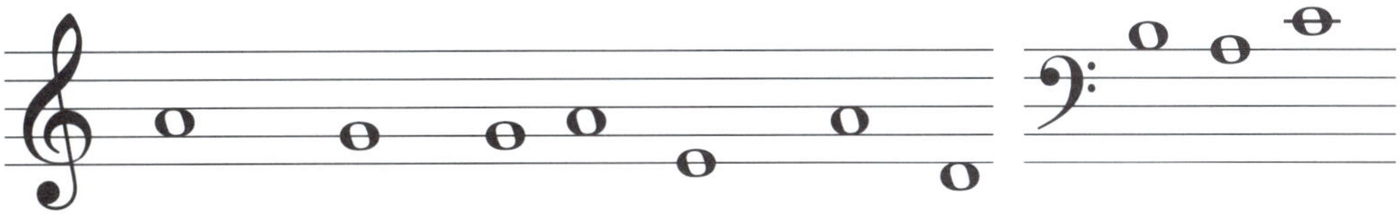

from the   st   rtin   t   n   k.

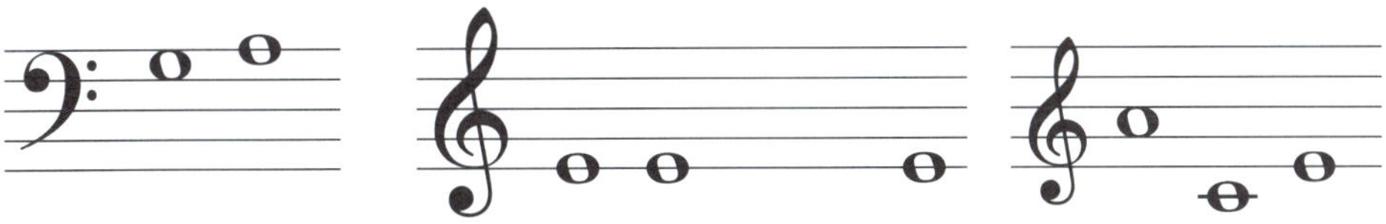

Press the   s to k   p th   p   ;

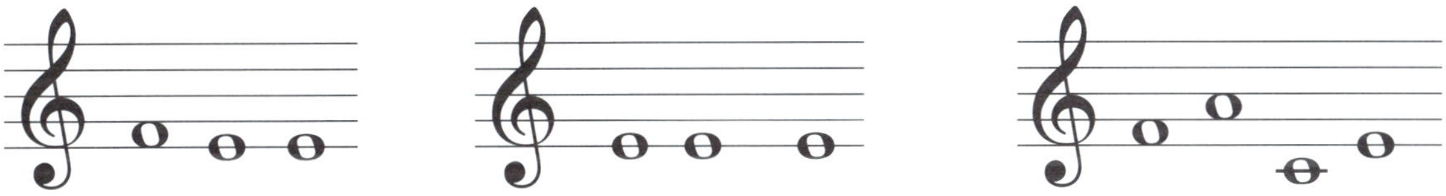

l the br   z   s in my   .

r   to make the cart   o   st;

pl   o hurry,   on't   l   st!

Use with Lesson Book 2, pg. 20

The Scrambler

A popular ride at *Piano Park* is the Scrambler.

1. Write the note names in the blanks.
2. In the blue boxes, rearrange the letters to spell words. On some staves, more than one word is possible.

Find the answers on page 18.

The Queen's Castle

To reach the top of the castle, Spike and Party Cat must write notes on the staff in each window.

Beginning on the ground floor, draw whole notes above the letter names on each staff. See how quickly you can reach the top of the tower.

Use with Lesson Book 2, pg. 23

Back to the Scrambler

Draw a whole note for each letter of the words below.

F A C E
(CAFE)

E D G E

B E A D

B A G
(GAB)

A G E

B A D
(DAB)

E G G

D E A F
(FADE)

Brass Fanfare

Trumpeters are sounding the call for everyone to come and see the *Piano Park* parade. One of the trumpeters plays one octave lower than the other.

1. Name the notes.
2. Write the melody one octave lower or higher than written.

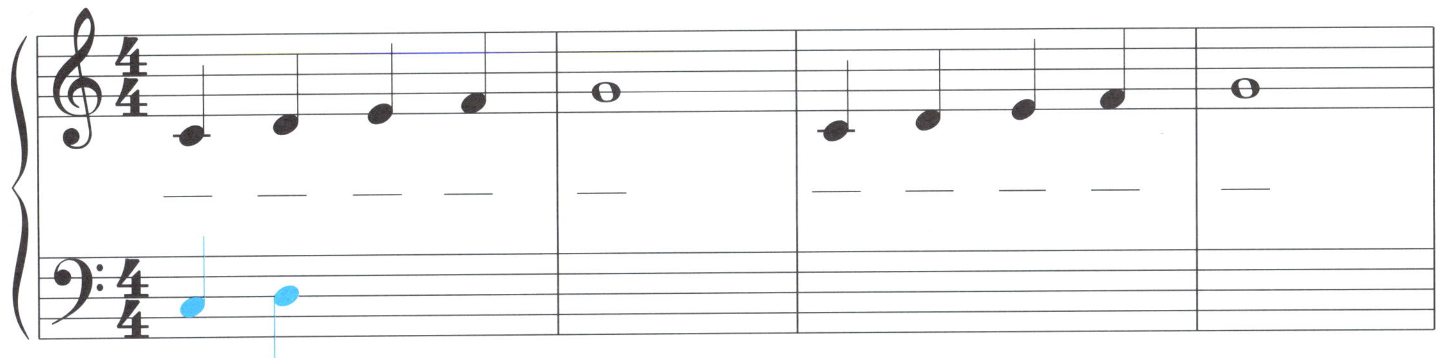

Use with Lesson Book 2, pg. 27

The Star Quest Ride

Name the notes to complete the story.

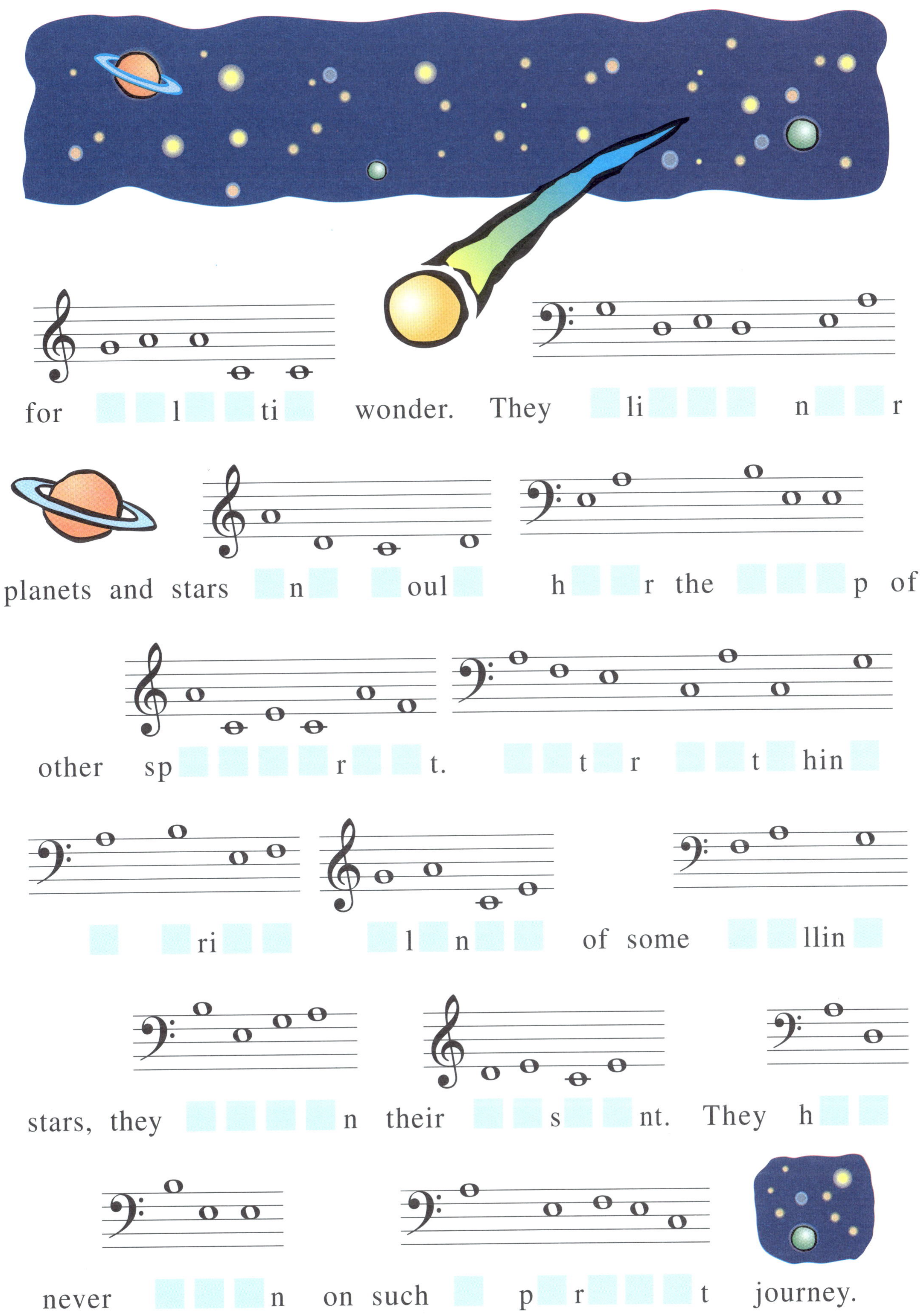

for   l   ti   wonder.   They   li   n   r
planets and stars   n   oul   h   r the   p of
other   sp   r   t.   t   r   t hin
ri   l   n   of some   llin
stars, they   n their   s   nt.   They   h
never   n on such   p   r   t   journey.

Star Quest Spaceships

On the Star Quest ride, Party Cat and Spike meet spaceships of all kinds.

1. Moving up by steps, draw two more quarter notes on each spaceship.
2. Add a sharp sign before each "F" note.
3. Write the note names in the boxes.

Haunted House

In the haunted house, Spike sees ghosts holding staves with note patterns. Each pattern has a matching one with the same intervals, but different notes. Before leaving the house, Spike must find the ghosts with the matching patterns.

1. Draw a line from each pattern on the left to the matching one on the right.
2. Write the note names in the blue boxes.
3. Circle all the 4ths.

Use with Lesson Book 2, pg. 34

The Sky Ride

From the sky ride, Party Cat and Spike can see all of *Piano Park*. The flags in the park are decorated with Treble Clef staves.

1. Draw whole notes to match the letter names on each flag.
2. Draw a sharp before the second note of each example.

The Submarine Ride

On the submarine ride, Spike and Party Cat see beautiful fish and a boat with sunken treasure. Along the watery trail are markers with Bass Clef staves.

1. Draw whole notes to match the letter names on each marker.
2. Draw a flat before each "B."

Use with Lesson Book 2, pg. 37

The Water Slide

Name the notes to complete the story.

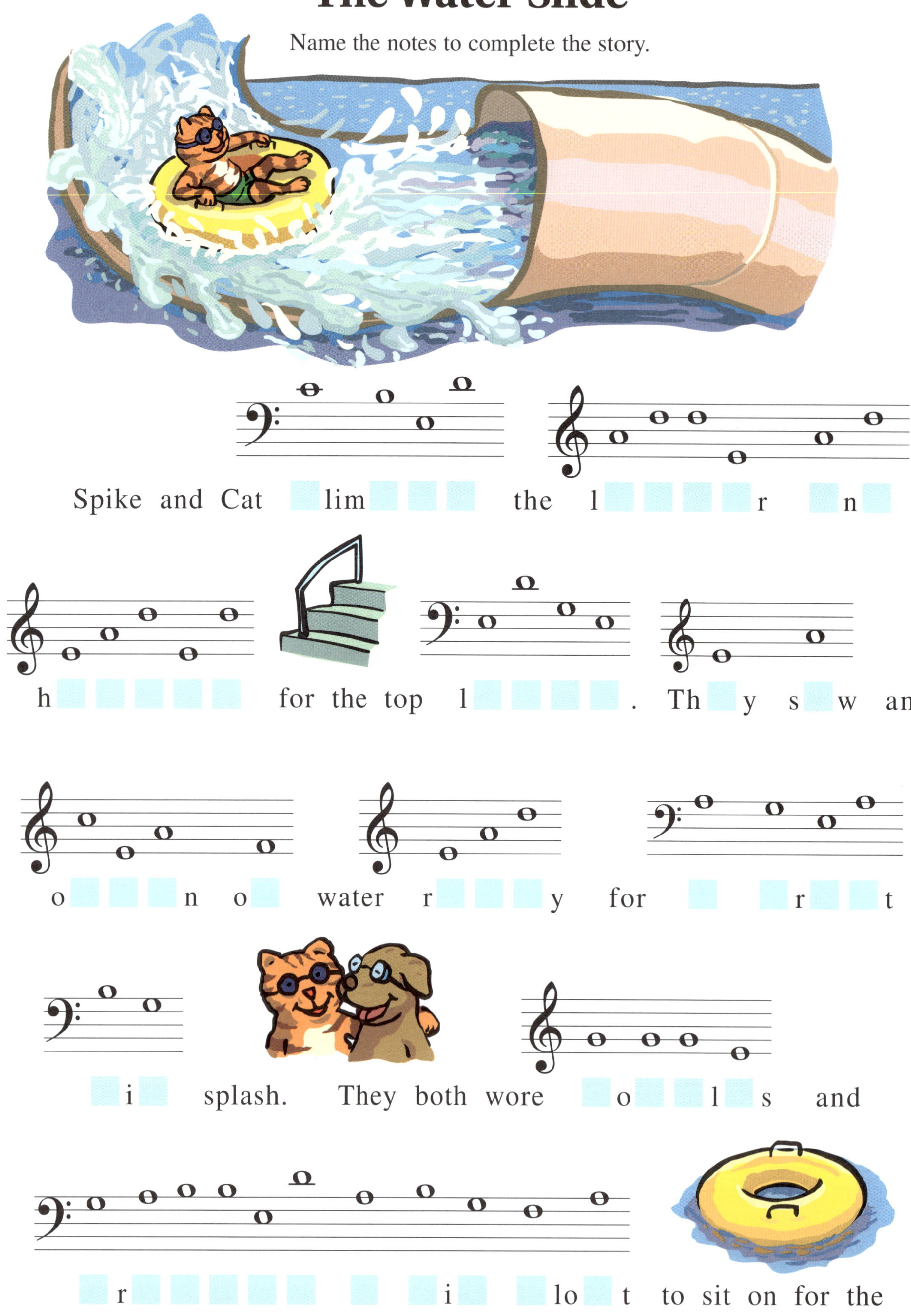

li   down.   Spike l   the way.   or
r   hin   the   p w t   r, they   li
past steep   n   s that m   them go   st   r
n   st   r.   or   long, they   m
i   nt   splash in the pool.   Wh   t   un!

Bumper Cars

This ride is one of Bear's favorites because he can drive the car by himself.
To make the engines start, he must first name and write some notes on the cars.

1. On each car, draw a quarter note that is one skip lower.
2. Name both notes.

The Merry-Go-Round

The *Piano Park* merry-go-round is decorated with different note patterns.

1. Name the notes in each pattern.
2. Draw a line to match each Treble Clef pattern to its Bass Clef twin.

Use with Lesson Book 2, pg. 44

The Roller Coaster

Name the notes to complete the story.

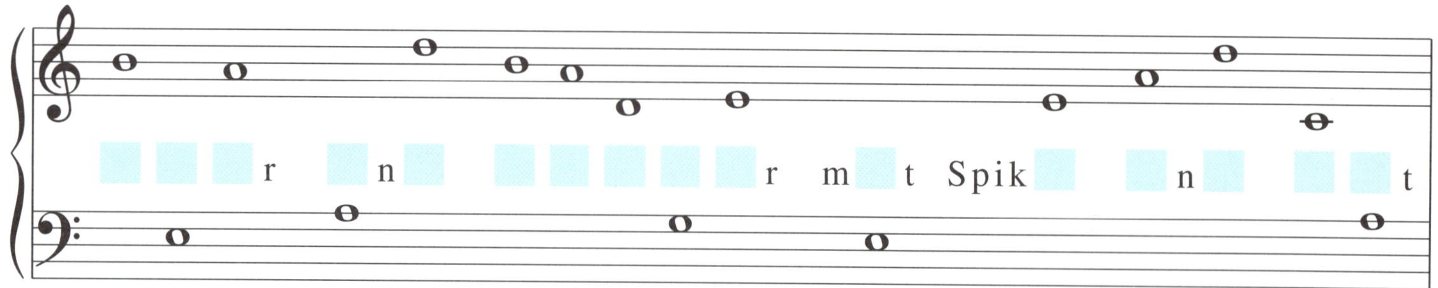

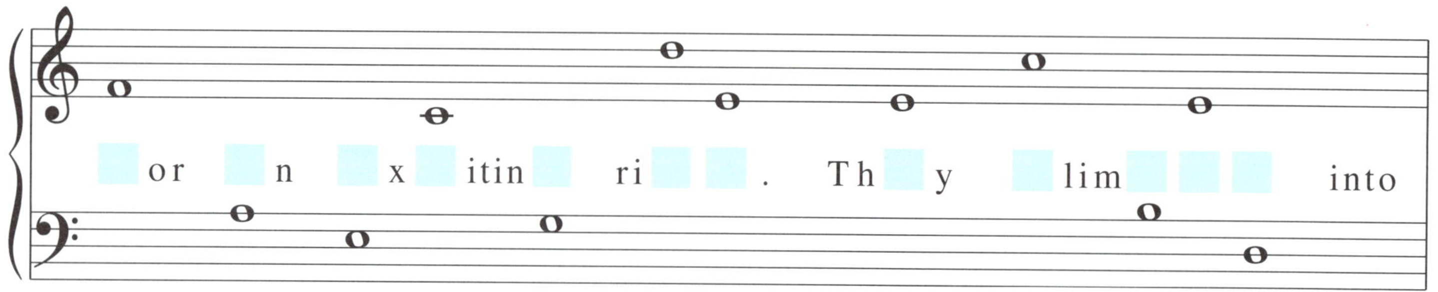

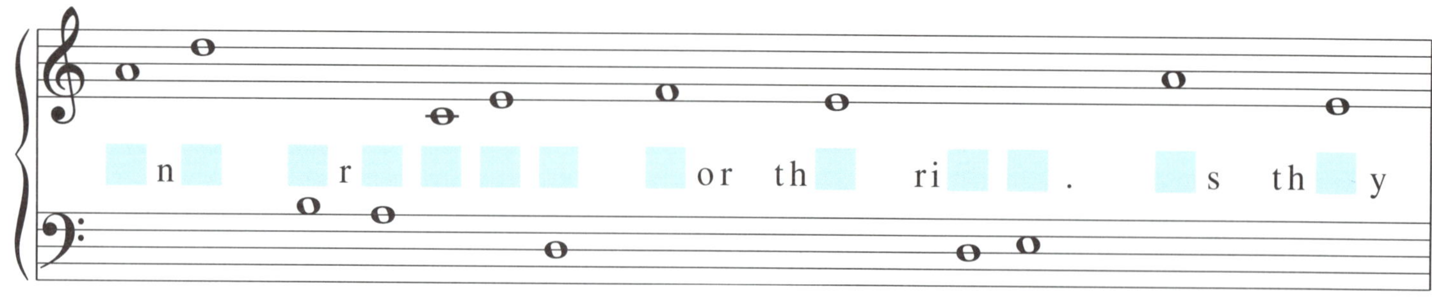

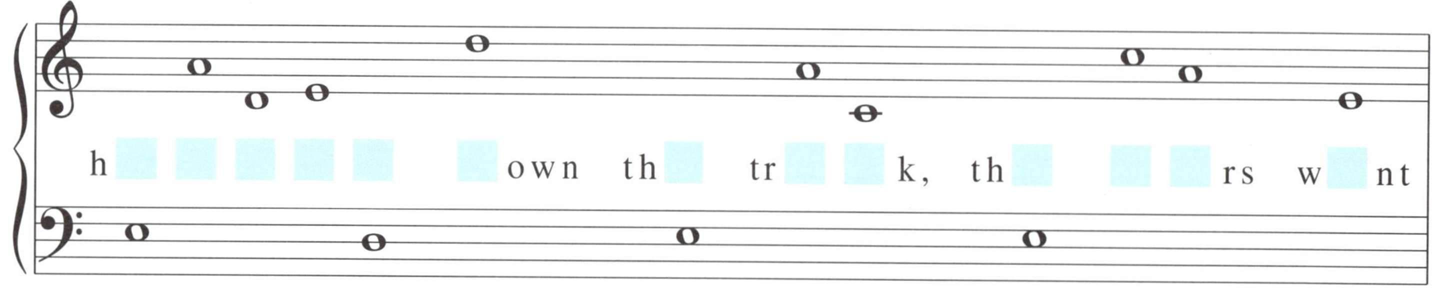

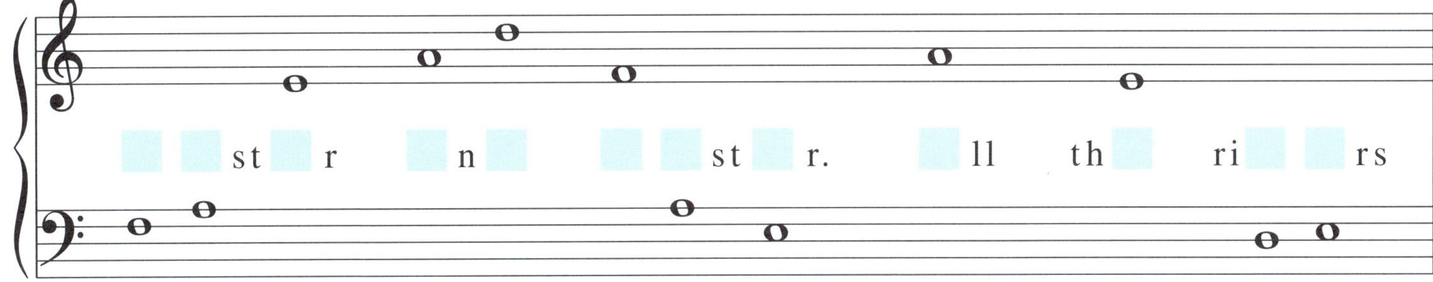
st   r   n   st r.   ll th ri   rs

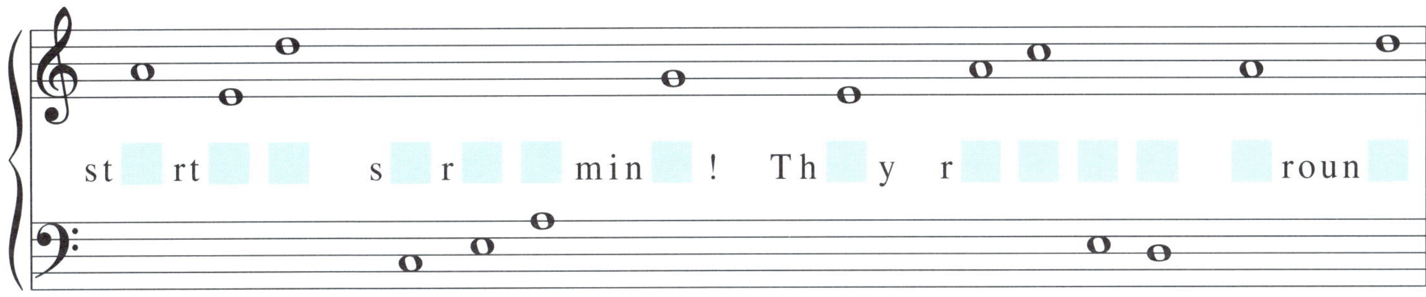
st rt   s r   min ! Th y r   roun

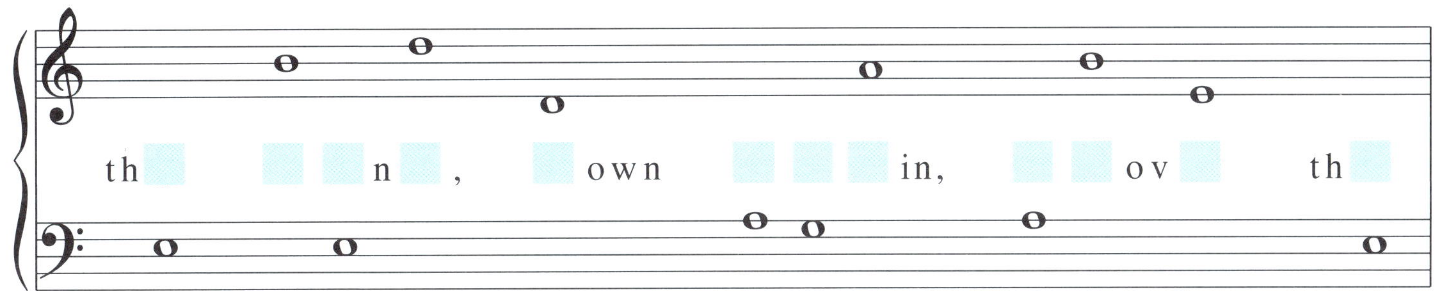
th   n ,   own   in,   ov   th

row   n   v n   lipp   upsi   own.

This   w s th   s ri st ri   v r!

Celebration

At the end of the day, *Piano Park* presents a laser light and fireworks show. Patterns of light fill the sky. The notes in the patterns name some of the attractions in *Piano Park*. Name the notes to spell names of the rides and games.

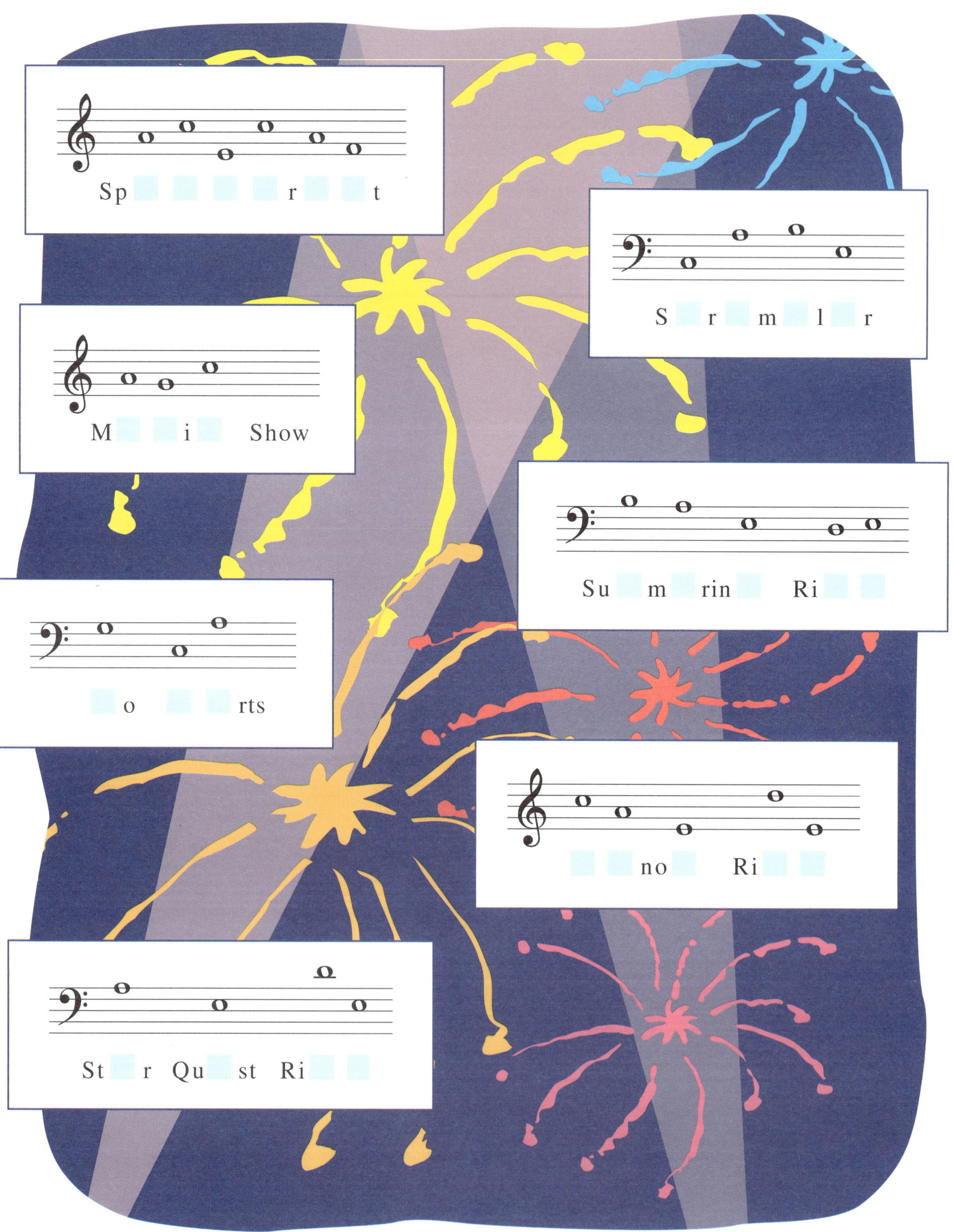